Cam and

Written by Isabel Thomas

Illustrated by Jennifer Naalchigar

Cam is sad to go.

Cam sat on the mat.

Tam sat on the mat.

Tam got a dot to dot.

It is a dog in a cap!

Talk about the story

Ask your child these questions:

1 Why was Cam sad at the beginning of the book?

2 What did Cam sit on?

3 What did Tam get?

4 Why was Cam happy at the end?

5 How do you do a 'dot to dot'?

6 What cheers you up if you're feeling sad?

Can your child retell the story using their own words?